Winter Journey

OTHER BOOKS BY TONY TOWLE

Poems (privately printed, 1966)

After Dinner We Take a Drive into the Night (Tibor de Nagy Editions, 1968)

North (Columbia University Press, 1970)

Lines for the New Year (Adventures in Poetry, 1975)

"Autobiography" and Other Poems (Sun/Coach House South, 1977)

Works on Paper (Swollen Magpie Press, 1978)

Gemini — collaborations with Charles North (Swollen Magpie Press, 1981)

New & Selected Poems (Kulchur Foundation, 1983)

Some Musical Episodes (Hanging Loose Press, 1992)

The History of the Invitation: New & Selected Poems 1963 – 2000 (Hanging Loose Press, 2001)

Memoir 1960 – 1963 (Faux Press, 2001)

Nine Immaterial Nocturnes (Barretta Books, 2003)

Winter Journey

Tony Towle

Hanging Loose Press
Brooklyn, New York

Published by Hanging Loose Press, 231 Wyckoff Street, Brooklyn, NY 11217. All rights reserved. No part of this book may be reproduced without the publisher's written permission, except for brief quotations in reviews.

Printed in the United States of America
10 9 8 7 6 5 4 3 2 1

Hanging Loose thanks the Literature Program of the New York State Council on the Arts for a grant in support of the publication of this book.

Some of these works first appeared in *The Mississippi Review, I Saw Johnny Yesterday, Poetry After 9-11* (Melville House, 2002), *Pataphysics, Hanging Loose, Nine Immaterial Nocturnes* (Barretta Books, 2003), *Sal Mimeo, Jacket* (on-line), *Milk* (on-line), T*he Poetry Project Newsletter, The Hat, Black Box* (on-line), *Voices of the City* (Hanging Loose, 2004), *180 More* (Random House, 2005), *Lit 10, The Duplications* (on-line), *The Best American Poetry 2006* (Scribner Poetry, 2006); "Scenes for Alexandra MacPherson Kelley" "Spring" and, from "Illuminations (Diverse Miniatures)": "On the River" "Prague" "Cenotaph" and "Envoy" were published in *Zoland Poetry*.

The quotations in "Dependable Epigraphs" are fictitious, except for that of Paul Valéry; Sigmund Freud's is accurate except for the addition of one word.

Re: line 24 of "Digression, 5/10/03," this 1959 benefit was for LeRoi Jones's magazine, *Yugen*.

Thanks to Michele Somerville for inspiring "Misprision."

These works were composed between 2000 and 2007.

Cover photo (rooftop, 81 Warren Street, 1981) by Jean Holabird.

Back cover photo by Diane Tyler.

Library of Congress Cataloging-in-Publication Data available on request.

 Produced at The Print Center, Inc. 225 Varick St., New York, NY 10014, a non-profit facility for literary and arts-related publications. (212) 206-8465

TABLE OF CONTENTS

for Kenneth Koch

In the Coffee House

the Mona Lisa, in the Village
at Bleecker and Seventh, a blip
from the middle ages
on the radar screen
of that young woman over there,
while she thinks of someone else.

I should have brought
something to read
because I have nothing to do now
but write, the way I used to
forty years ago, in the Figaro
in the Village
at Bleecker and MacDougal, exhilarated
by loneliness, poverty, and paralyzing
indecision, resolutely ignoring the fact
that everyone cool in there
knew that I wasn't —
lost to what was *happening*
behind the overpriced coffee, 35 cents
for the fuel
to infiltrate oblivion;

and I waited for a girlfriend
and composed jejune little ironies
that I hoped would pass for poems
and I had all the time in the world.

*

The San Remo bar was there across the street
where I learned years later
real New York poets went
and drank real drinks,
but the San Remo is gone
with everything else from 1960 —
discarded, lost, or broken, or certainly

wouldn't fit anymore,
except for the sound advice
still gathering dust:

Think before you speak.
(Yes, I probably should have done that.)
A penny saved is a penny earned.
(That could have been made a bit clearer, perhaps.)
Don't be a complete *idiot.*
(Hey, I gave it a shot.)
You should really think about a career.
I'm thinking about it now
and there it is: unintentional barbs,
unasked-for opinions
and missed opportunities strewn
and rusting about the incorporeal field.

I told Diane I'd be here 'til six. Waiting
for a girlfriend *literally* is a great improvement
over the afternoons at the Figaro;
and in fact it's cool to *have* a girlfriend at my age
I think amusedly to myself
behind the overpriced coffee —
2.95 to contemplate the traffic
fleeing down the avenue and into the past
which has brought me up to the present,
where I put down my pen, figuratively.

BAGATELLE

Clouds have again
seized control of the weekend
and Teshub, storm god of the Hittites
(Toshiba, according to the SpellCheck)
casually mentions, in a moistened Aramaic
(which is odd, because it is not
his first language, nor
as you might suppose, is it mine)
that we're really in for it this time,
that *liquidity* will be a daily
fact of life for the rest of the year
which means, he explains, that in addition
to the endless rain, cosmic investors
could turn in our world to make a profit
at the planetary exchange —
or more likely to cut a loss.
Since I have already removed the helmet of judgment
I will check on the proceedings in Orange County
where "Tony Towle" is suing David M. Reyneaud,
et al., for automotive negligence. It seems
that Dave and those other bastards out there
tried to run down the last persona
I can afford to maintain in Southern California,
my liquidity being what it is,
not that he ever supplies any interesting imagery —
just sits on the beach all day and stares at the ocean
in a vast impression of liquidity,
a Mr. Hulot's Holiday without the verbosity,
which is exactly the kind of reference
that sails right over his head and plunks into the Pacific
and that he thinks must have been a fish.
By now I'm on a trip, if not exactly a vacation
though I anticipate brambles, mosquitoes,
poisonous berries and lunatics with shotguns
as I usually encountered on vacation,
except when I would sit on the beach
and consider the Great North Atlantic,

investing the feeling
that vacations would last longer
than I knew they were going to. But it seems Teshub,
as is the way with storm gods, was hyperbolizing
for the rain has finally stopped;
Apollo has opened another referential window
and is beginning to apply sunlight to the moisture.
"Have a swell apotheosis," Teshub tells me
and, startled, before I can manage a "Thanks, you too"
we are parted by the clearing air.

HYPOTHESES

Imagine turning the clock back
to when there were no clocks,
and then back another hour and a half
just to make sure. Imagine the unique insights
your wristwatch will give you, even though it is running slow.
Imagine how you will feel if it stops.

This brochure invites us to imagine
reliving the terrors of World War II,
but the explosions are deafening and it seems hazardous,
so we come back. Instead, let's imagine a bright blue Mesopotamian sky
and the peaceful Baghdad of January 1258
with the Mongols somewhere in the distance.
Imagine trying to explain to the Caliph what's going to happen
when they get there, that his grand vizier is double-crossing him,
that the city's inhabitants will be slaughtered,
that he will be mocked at a banquet and then he and his sons
will be sewn into carpets and trampled by the Mongol horsemen.
The description will become unimaginably gruesome
so imagine that you are a peacefully falling leaf that is, like,
kind of, actually, you know, floating in a present-day
colloquial breeze, or whatever, while there I remain,
real or imagined, inside behind the autumnal window,
unraveling the sizeless sweater of the unknown
into countless piles of yarn. You wander off to seek advice
from the symbolically obscure but kindly old welder,
whose torch, like an indulged nephew or sputtering oracle
perched on his remaining knee
spits out an indefatigable stream of chromatic enlightenment,
and within the vanishing sparks
you are imagined as just a normal person
facing an enormous stack of bills
that require payment for everything you've ever imagined.
Imagine you have the money to take care of them all.
Imagine what will happen when they find out you don't,
and they resort to the unimaginable: sending grim reality
to infiltrate your imagination.

CLASH OF ARTISTIC TEMPERAMENTS

You see, Plutarch
used to call poetry
"noisy dancing" whereas
I think of dancing
as sweaty poetry,
indoors under the hot
prosodic lights, feet
all over the place, but
remembering to hold
the capricious words just
far enough away
to keep them respectably unaware
of my arousal.

NINE IMMATERIAL NOCTURNES

En el Viejo México

First, you gut the burrito, for then events will proceed.
You were to uncover the señorita's repressed desires
and then get the *infierno* out of there
before she uncovered yours; but
it was too late and, if not exactly history
at least the perpetuation of unreality
in another language:
the *perro* chasing you for effect, a *cabeza*
mouthing imprecations from the window
that will reconstruct for you,
your worship, the streets that come to their end
in the comedy of finding and losing,
in the schemes of diamonds, ovals, circles
sparkling beneath the blue parlor of miles
and the fictive arrows that arrive from her female glance
still pointed.

Hudson and Worth

As the car alarms disconcertingly
respond to each other's pitch
I look down the former Anthony Street,
a former Anthony myself, where the moon
is full on the ears of Leon the donkey
and the hibiscus tree remains untamed
but picturesque and leaning a little forward
as if to peek between the curtains to the asphalt below,
where a diagram of the 1943 Battle of Kursk has been laid out
in myriad notations of red and orange.
Notice the red arrows near the parking lot. They
are Rossokovsky's T-34's, which will pierce the German salient.
At sunrise, faculty from a military college
will utilize jackhammers to simulate the clamor of battle
while we huddle in our bunkers until the lesson is complete.

Le Voyage

Every little breeze
takes on import
during Hurricane Awareness Week
which has kicked off
another Real Estate Avarice Month
here in fashionable Tribeca,
where this evening my voices have informed me
that my French isn't *good* enough to save France
(though my accent is certainly better than theirs);
but I wasn't trying to save France,
I wanted to save money to *go* to France. We can
air these and other topics of internalized interest
as I continue on down the street,
since the passersby assume I am on an unseen cell phone,
a bilingual conference call of schizophrenic significance.

Prospects

I would like to live long enough
to see the State Quarters Program
clink to a successful conclusion,
twelve dollars and fifty cents of wealth and history
fulfilled in elegant cardboard circles;
but now the premise takes off in a different direction,
for as Kentucky was about to fork over its two bits
for a second admission to the Union,
the imps of haphazard historicity
subjected the skyline to the whims of religious psychopaths;
and before that I had never purchased an American flag —
since I always knew where I *was* and, when abroad
(at least in England), the natives always knew where I was *from* —
but in October I bought two: from immigrants
making a tenuous living, appropriately,
from Africa and Asia, respectively
and on Wall Street, no less.

Archive

Social realists throw themselves into networking
while impressionists drift into scenarios,
where at the moment Catherine the Great draws nearer,
her Russo-Teutonic bosom heaving
with antique but passionate monumentality.
Fabricated trepidation has never before been this animated
I surmise, but the empress is coming to resemble
Margaret Dumont, and thus my anxiety
increases significantly. But let me just move on
and say that in my next impression
the aliens have affirmed their evil intentions
and the death dust is entering the chamber,
yet there is an absence of detail
except for the picturesque Alpine village
and, because it sounds as if the containers
are coming loose again, we put on our capes and fly there.

Shelf Life

After putting *New! The Wisdom of Ancient Egypt*
back with the Oxymoronic Releases,
and leaving *Small Arms of the World*
and *Be Your Own Dick* unperused
in the bin marked Please Don't Judge Books by Their Titles,
I come across Steve Levine's *What Brooklyn Means to Me*
on its own unlabeled shelf,
while my recent *General Annoyance*
has been included under "Military Biography, French."
But back to reality, as the store is getting ready to close:
I pick up a copy of *Medieval Ways to Have Fun*
in case I am ever back that way, and the
Love Your Heart Cookbook: The Aztec Way to Healthy Eating,
with its accompanying high-decibel audiotape
and "how-to" glyphs
for the audacious chef.

Ethos

Vous êtes un de ces types Protestants qui
se trouve seulement à Genève
(You are one of those Protestant types
one finds only in Geneva)
I overheard an older man saying lasciviously to a young one
at the Cedar Bar a very long time ago
in clear, textbook French and I was startled,
apprehensive for a second that it had been directed at me,
though I have never been to Geneva —
and I don't think that's what Calvin had in mind
when *he* went to Geneva; he went to create an ethos,
through which as a distant subtextual consequence
I find myself engaged in marginally necessary yardwork
somewhere between Olivebridge and Krumville
to justify midnight sensuality later on,
in the waters of the enchanted spring
with *Dian*, the woodland nymph
who conveyed me here from the metropolis
by means of a spirited white Toyota.
But work for reward is not what Calvin meant either,
really, yet it is out of his control, isn't it,
for that's what happens to an ethos: it dapples the landscape
like invisible confetti from a distant century,
falling unobserved as one rakes the leaves,
gathers the kindling.

Diptych

Cactus poachers work quickly
and we cactuses know it;
keeping our spines
sticking straight out all night
is an effort well worth it
when we hear a curse and feel a drop of blood;
then our "eyes" twinkle in the depth
of our anthropomorphized pulp
on the giant land mass veiled here and there
by these dabs of metamorphosis,
as I imagine myself in that space,
planted before a background of tropical dots,
or I imagine myself in *that* space, dropping
through the exploded event
of powdered electricity and pulverized death.
And I could tell you more about life on my planet
since I will get tired of just standing here:
our oxygen needs are simple, but we force wit,
laughter and subtlety to carry gloom,
lamentation and humorlessness on their shoulders.

Phenomena

"With holidays around the corner
you can sweep easily through the words
of a talented writer," the critic said
but not of me, alas. "With hardly a festival in sight
you can briskly ignore irrelevant idiosyncrasy
and pointless rhapsodizing"
would be more like it;
but nobody's poetry is any good
until someone in prose says it is,
and writes out a check and bestows a certificate;
others, milling ambiguous in the shadows,
say nothing. The trick
is not to care. The trick is,
from my precarious pseudo-aeropagite
perch on the sofa, with the traditional
insulating glove of blubber worn down to nothing,
to reach yet again into the icy water
at the bottom of the room
and find additional specimens
no one will see.

THE DINNER PARTY

Ah, life is a reassuring dream that is vivid but comfortably mundane, said the shmuck aloud to himself as he sat down next to the shlemiel and indulged in an expansive gesture of certitude that sent the latter's soup into the lap of the adjacent shlimazel. The shmendrick apologized, to no one in particular, and the shmegeggy accepted; while the shlep scuffled off to the kitchen to get another bowl, and at the front door the shnorrer pushed past the shlumps to talk his way in. It was the putz, of course, that had arranged the seating, which included a decorous mélange of shmoes crowded in next to the radiator, sweating and uncomfortable but grateful to have been invited. I have no idea where I'm supposed to sit, so I leave and go sit in the park — where I hear an avian voice: "Hey, you don't recognize me? I'm the pigeon that craps on your windowsill. Why are you down here in the cold when you could be upstairs eating a free meal? What are you, some kind of *shnook*?"

ANTHROPOMORPHIC ETIQUETTE

1
When a monkey courts a dragon
he must never arrive at her lair
with a gift less bizarre
than the impending relationship.

2
At the fête, the female goat
should caper with the snake before the rat
and thereafter the ox, but leave with the dog
for he will relish her credentials.

3
If you are a male goat
stay right where you are
but eventually gravitate toward the arts
for then you will be the goat of her dreams.

4
The female horse should resist rearing up
with passionate hooves before a favored guest,
thus upsetting the delicate equilibrium
and the trough.

5
When a male rabbit calls on a female tiger
it is improper that he be startled by the doorbell
and scamper back down the hall to the elevator,
after having requested the rendezvous.

6
The female rooster should always follow her instincts
and then perhaps apologize for the misunderstanding.

GEMINI

May 21st

Fragrant groves of yuzu
as we gaze at the prospect

opening the chamber
for inspection

Keep it short

May 22nd

It is depressing to find out
your friends
are as depressed
as you are

May 23rd

Seriously
the opera guides
the star to practice
no more notes
than today
will elucidate

Susan says hello,
cloaked
for example

May 24th

"I always feel happy
when I find a pretty dim sum
in a steaming basket"
says Kageyama-san
memorably

May 25th

in due course, a handsome tomb,
a rosebush, it is said
of the loonies

in spectacular thorny
settings popping
up acutely

The destruction of Dallas

May 26th

again, resembles
the rose

extravagant morbidity,

leave your business
to the catacombs

May 27th

teeth going to hell

May 28th

The unread book hanging
loosely in the riverine moat
faces more peril from within

its character contradictory

but learn this:
scruples and opinions
retard the career
and are of no use whatever
to the merchant classes

May 29th

Internal couriers bring advice
that in some sense
must be considered
Towle-esque

May 30th

composed
of inward promptings,
if you will, otherwise
no data

May 31st

Stay up there

oh pitted lunar grape

June 1st

Looking closely at the photo
of the motorboat caught at the peak
of a five-thousand-foot wave,
there is a black dot on the bow I know
to be a fly, the same one that is here
now. I get in the boat and re-create
this event to make sure
it could happen, for it is truly
amazing to see the craft fall
back into the sea without
damage and that the fly has survived
and I am the only one to have noticed.

June 2nd

My gloves were
on the red stool
of course, not
a tree stump
somewhere

June 3rd

In the airport bar a woman
I didn't want to notice me
notices me (*I think she was supposed
to be the woman who confided to me
once in Puffy's that she had also had
a tumble with the sous-chef that Jean
had a very public affair with and which
gave the coup de grâce to our break-up.
Not only did she favor me with this
information but seemed to think I would
find it appealing and gave the impression
that consequently she*

would like to go to bed with me,
too, and I was thinking: if there
was ever a chance before,
sweetheart, you just pulverized it with
that gratuitous little confidence) —
while the planes articulate around
the runways like pythons
and it is clear that if only I could
find the schedule for Poulenc's
Oboe Sonata I could get
on a flight and leave this place.

June 4th

Oxymoronically
I gave myself
a good
poke in the eye

June 5th

One-eyed Odin was
bad tempered
too

June 6th

Health, strength, and vitality
would be nice

June 7th

a picture of composure
on the doorstep of destiny

I'm not myself today

June 8th

Down to Wall Street,
giant sea mammals
slapping the water
in front of us
to clear the way

Don't ask

June 9th

celebration, subdued
I imagine
on 92nd Street

June 10th

no reliable data

June 11th

Hello? Answer the telephone,

not zombies

"I thought you left"

"Yeah I did, but my bag
is still here."

Elinor Nauen
should be mentioned

June 12th

ah, youth

June 13th

I can't seem to find anything

June 14th

How many meteors?

About a thousand,
if the screen is wide

Her breasts
are her bread and butter,
apparently, as unlikely
as that sounds

June 15th

Spain? No, the hungry wolf

You still haven't answered
the question

called away on business

June 16th

Granted, what's
your second wish?

June 17th

Happy Birthday Ron Padgett
and Venus Williams,
though little is known about them

June 18th

nothing so far (3:55 p.m.)

but this photograph

June 19th

just more work

June 20th

gone

is Chairman Ed

                    above

a sign
  moving on

                                 May – June 2003

Dependable Epigraphs

*My epigraphs will prepare you for the excursion
but not for the ruts in the road.*

— Virgil

Stay well ahead of your turnips in the garden of life.

— Michel de Montaigne

Never parade your ignorance; a discreet amble down a side street will suffice.

— Benjamin Disraeli

Don't swat flies close to the ear of God.

— St. Francis of Assisi

Metaphors are the unstable companions of an already impractical fellow.

— Henry Ford

*Those who are not willing to subvert the law do not have sufficient stake in
the outcome of events.*
— Niccolò Machiavelli

If patriotism is the last refuge of a scoundrel, religion is certainly the first.

— Voltaire

Everywhere I go I find a poet has already been there neurotically before me.

— Sigmund Freud

Socializing is networking to no purpose.

— Oscar Wilde

Politics is the art of preventing people from taking part in affairs which properly concern them.

— Paul Valéry, as quoted in the original French at a press conference by George W. Bush

Farewell, O insatiable biographers of the future.

— William Shakespeare

Pimp my soporific and annoying orchestral arrangements, bitch!

— Lawrence Welk

The peasant's place is in the hovel.

— Harry & Leona Helmsley

The woman's place is in the novel.

— Henry James

Never let Henry James have the last word.

— Edith Wharton

You've got to know when to stop.

— Leo Tolstoy

The Investigation

I found myself in the Great Central Library reachable through the labyrinthine passages from either the East Side or Sixth Avenue subways. I had forgotten all about this enormous complex because I had spent time here only once, in one of the larger rooms that was further ahead, for research in a job that didn't work out some years before. But now I was walking purposefully among the high and dusty bookcases that had no visible organization, and suddenly in front of me on a shelf at eye-level were a number of well-known poetry reference books. This orange-covered volume I have at home, but this one, *A Measure of Poets*, I knew about but had never bought because, to my distress, I was not in it.

Nonetheless, I took it down, on the possibility that somehow I might have been included in the index. "If I'm not in this thing at all," I thought to myself, "then that's *it* . . . " leaving the implication unvocalized. But there were indeed several citations about me; quite a few, in fact — references in articles about other poets — and more appeared as I looked. And then there was a full-page photograph I had completely forgotten about — a long-distance shot taken in the middle of an invented Grand Central Station that was part of the enormous subway-library structure where I was at that very moment: I am the only occupant of a large, circular, leather banquette, and am leaning back with my right arm extended over the empty platform behind the seats, in a staged and allegorical pose I recalled having to hold uncomfortably long for the camera; and I am in the act of throwing from a cup objects like dice, which the camera had caught in mid-air.

Around me was my "family" — two children, actors, in front on the right, and a woman I didn't recognize, gathered together for the purpose of the tableau, and a young man a little way off who was supposed to be my brother, and who moved himself a few steps further to the left as I examined the picture, to improve the overall composition. Behind this grouping was the station's enormous back wall of marble, at least fifty feet high — and beige, I think, although the photo was in black and white — or even higher, as I held the book at arm's length so I could appreciate the full expanse of the panoramic scene. But what was the game I was in the act of exemplifying so dramatically? I peered intently at the tiny objects flying out of the cup. "Hazard" kept coming to mind, but that was a card game, I told myself, and what I was tossing from the cup were three-dimensional symbols that in my pose I could not quite turn my head to comprehend.

DIGRESSION, 5/10/03

"for" Joe LeSueur

Listening to Samuel Barber's
orchestrated Souvenirs of whatever it was
he was remembering with the Mets on the tube
with the sound off would be an oxymoronic
afternoon to some, even a gender-preference tussle,
or manly brawl, but to others — me —
a way of building up the entertainment quotient
before adding actual *activity* to the mix,
perhaps editing for those who will give me money,
or laboring over my own work
when *I'm* the one who pays; and the Mets
are like an orchestra in need of rehearsal not
like the ensemble playing "Sam's"
exquisite miniature song for oboe,
the most beautiful instrument I think
even though I have never heard
a 20th-century piano concerto I didn't like,
a coincidence of sensibility I shared with Frank
although mercifully neither one of us
had to hear them all. And you left out
a great story that you told me back in '64
which you said Frank didn't like to talk about
of how at the Living Theatre reading five years before,
which *wasn't* the LeRoi Jones benefit by the way —
that was in '63 and I was there — because LeRoi
was one of the readers in this one, with Allen
and Ray Bremser; there is a famous *Voice* photo
of the three of them watching Frank read that Larry used
in a lithograph, incorporating Frank's "To a Young Poet,"
about John Weiners — so Frank was reading that poem
and others and Kerouac was in the audience,
drunk, and yelling: "Get off the stage, O'Hara, you faggot,
I want to read some haiku!" and after a few minutes of this
Frank actually started to leave but the audience
said: "No, don't go, don't listen to him"

and so forth but Kerouac wouldn't stop and finally
Frank, walking off, said, "No, that's all right, let him read,
my silence is more interesting than his bullshit" —
though delivered, as you told me, with tears in his eyes.

Well, like the Mets I'm coming up to bat
in the bottom of the 9th, or maybe the 8th, if I'm lucky
but far behind in the game —
and the music seems to have stopped to listen.

1346 Redux

When I first dipped into Froissart's chronicle of the Battle of Crécy
(Cray-CEE, I eventually learned), the first major land engagement
of the Hundred Years War, I was nine, and even
through the wondrous panoply of imagined knightly warfare
was given pause when the mercenary Genoese crossbowmen
were *discomfited* by the relentless showers of English arrows —
fired from a range they could not match, their own bowstrings
being wet from a momentary downpour, and having just marched
eighteen tiring miles to get there, and the French king
was then so insensitive and precipitate as to order them
immediately forward to "soften up" the English forces.

Not only were they discomfited, but *sorely vexed*
for when they were unwise enough to attempt to retire out of range
the Count of Alençon, considering this maneuver unacceptable
declared them to be *rascals*, and ordered mounted men-at-arms
to critique their performance with variously shaped medieval tools
(the *arms*), all of them designed to cause pain when applied with force,
even though these "monitors" were now
getting first-hand experience of discomfiture themselves
as the English archers had neither the manners nor wit to distinguish
between hirelings and their betters — so that the crossbowmen
must have indulged in the most pungent colloquialisms
available to the 14th-century Genoese dialect,
which I will attempt to approximate: *Ouch! another of those discomfiting*
pointed missiles seems to be penetrating the protective garments
meant to keep them out. Considering that, to say the least, these French
are not sympathetic to our issues, in fact are participating
in diminishing our numbers to an alarming degree, and, as employers,
are clearly impossible to please, was taking on this assignment
really the best use we could have made of our time and skill set?

TRUTH IN ADVERTISING

1. *On the Road*

The segmented demigod "Michelin Man"
who cushions our daily journeys, distributes
diminutive likenesses of himself, the votive figurines
we utilize on the road, to keep in touch
with his wisdom and pliability —
as in such manner were fashioned statuettes of *Gudea*
ruler of Bronze Age Sumerian *Lagash*
to call attention to his reality when not in personal view.
One day, "Michelin Man," resting in his automotive
conveyance, notices an acolyte who has paused
in his own vehicle to mistreat one of these benevolent effigies,
shaking it with violence and leering with menace,
as if to do it harm. The scoundrel looks up and sees
with chagrin who it is that has discovered
his execrable behavior. And how does "Michelin Man"
punish this impiety? Does he seize the blasphemer
and lock him in his trunk? No, he gazes down
sorrowfully, in quiet pity, so *resilient* is his compassion.

2. A Sunny Day

A man washing his car on a sunny day is approached
by two gangsters, who wordlessly "suggest" that he use
their cleaning product. Intimidated, he switches.
Interestingly, the thugs' merchandise seems to be quite effective
although it is not clear how much it will cost. Probably
quite a bit, because it seems that "protection" is included:
When a bulldog trots up to the car's rear wheel and lifts a leg
to pee on a tire the man has just washed, the mobsters
reach into their jackets as if to draw pistols and "blow away"
the offending animal. Sensing the danger, the dog
ambles off to relieve himself in safety somewhere else,
leaving the men in one of those overly complex scenarios
he has noticed humans so often find themselves.

3. The Evils of Drink

A man who is an alcoholic has disembarked from a plane
and is about to leave the airport. He sees a car service driver
holding up a sign with a doctor's name on it. Impetuously,
the man presents himself to the driver as that doctor, hoping
the car will be a limousine and have a bar as part of its amenities.
It is and does. Strangely, of the wide variety of beverages available,
the man chooses to drink only the most common brand of light beer.
He drinks quickly and has consumed enough to become fairly
inebriated by the time the car arrives at the hospital, where it seems
he is expected to perform brain surgery; that is, after he has paid the
driver eighty dollars, which he does not have. The situation quickly
becomes awkward. By the time the real doctor arrives by taxi
an hour later, the patient has died. In prison, the man makes a vow
that he will never drink that brand of light beer again.

4. Vehicular Presentiment

The Pathfinder has again come to that section
in the narrow cliffside road where it must drive over
the colossal letters of its own name, arranged backwards,
deeply incised in the stone — bumping down and up,
straining the suspension while moving carefully along
over the autobiographical roadway: from the I to the F,
and then across the H and the T, inching onto the edge of the A,
toward the perilous gap on the other side,
the hollowed-out space below the bulge of the P
into which the left front wheel will drop once more
and send the car plummeting into the bottomless canyon below —
and at this point the vehicle awakens, its cold engine shuddering
in the silent showroom, beads of moisture covering the hood,
the sales staff gone home for the night,
the stars twinkling above the beckoning mountains.

5. An Opera

A short, repellent, balding man who hates the opera is attending one. His sister, who is in the company, is singing an aria. Suddenly jealous, the man improvises a plan to deflect the audience's attention to himself. He walks calmly onto the stage, takes the microphone, and announces that the state's lottery jackpot is forty million dollars. Seized by uncontrollable avarice, the audience rises as one and rushes out to buy lottery tickets. The man smirks cynically, pleased to see proof of what he had always suspected: that greed will triumph over the pretentiousness of art. He remains on stage overlooking the empty seats, contemplating the satisfying power his few and simple words had had on so many. In the meantime, his sister has run off in humiliation, while the rest of the cast is struck dumb by the man's effrontery. A few minutes later, the patrons, having discovered the lottery payout that week was to be a mere four million, storm back into the theatre, incensed, intent on giving the exaggerator a sound thrashing or worse. Desperate to forestall his impending doom, with a cohort of silent Wagnerian extras as a backdrop, the man bursts pleadingly into song.

6. Irresistible Impulse

An equivocally oriented young man finds himself alone in a clothing store. He stares fascinated at a smooth, milky-white, faceless male mannequin until, on an erotic whim, he slips off the figure's jeans and puts them on himself, leaving his own trousers behind a counter. As he slips out of the store unnoticed, he senses that his act has teased the mannequin into existence. He walks slowly home, an occasional furtive glance showing him that indeed he is being followed by a white, featureless body clad only in boxer shorts. It has begun to rain. The young man goes into his apartment, closing the door behind him, leaving it unlocked. He lies down on the sofa and pretends to sleep. The rain is now a downpour beating against the windows and there are claps of thunder. The young man hears the door open and a few seconds later knows that the figure is standing over him. Eyes still closed, he feels himself becoming aroused, but he has not the slightest notion of what the inhuman mannequin intends to do.

7. A Lesson in Manners

Two men are having lunch in an outdoor café. When the bill arrives, one is eager to pay because the credit card he intends using offers extremely favorable terms. The other man points out that, actually, *his* credit card has a lower rate over the long run. The first man looks a little crestfallen, realizing that he doesn't have such a good deal after all. This should be the least of his worries. In the interim, a dozen or so men dressed as ninth-century marauders have surreptitiously wheeled a catapult up behind him, with the tip of the throwing arm extending beneath his chair. The man on the other side of the table gives no indication that untoward activity is taking place — he perhaps feels some reprimand is in order for the display of such tacky enthusiasm over a credit card. At any rate, one of the viking-esque ruffians cuts the catapult's restraining rope with his sword and in mid-sentence the credit-card enthusiast is hurtled instantly backwards a hundred feet in the air. His chair falls onto the roof of a parked car several blocks away, causing considerable damage. The man smashes like a watermelon against the side of a building, having traveled about half a mile in a very short time. As the jokesters wheel their device away, a faint smile crosses the face of the man left at the table. He feels satisfied that a point about good manners has been made. The smile fades a little when he grasps that now he himself must take care of the sizeable check the other man had been only too willing to pay.

8. A Chance Encounter

A living snowman is waiting for his scarf to dry in a laundromat.
He opens the door of the dryer to retrieve it but someone walks by
and carelessly hits the door, knocking the snowman into the drum.
Then an archetypal "hot young woman," in tank top and shorts,
oblivious that the machine is "occupied," opens the door, proceeds
to throw in her own clothes, starts the dryer, and sits down to wait.
One can see through the machine's window that the intense heat
has melted the snow from the snowman's bones and that his skeleton
and the lumps of coal that compose his face are all that's left as he
spins entangled with the woman's clothes. He manages to get out of
the dryer, however, just as she is raising a bottled potion to her lips.
He snatches the bottle away and drinks the contents down himself.
The miraculous coldness of the liquid causes the snowy "flesh" to
reappear on his body. But something is causing him discomfort. He
reaches into the packed snow of his thoracic sphere and pulls out a
purple brassiere, belonging to the young woman. He hands it to her.
The fact that an article of her lingerie has spent time inside this
creature seems to make the woman kittenish and sexually receptive,
and she gazes at the snowman with unmistakable passion. The latter,
now that he is back to normal, gives her a wicked and seductive smile.
But he knows perfectly well that a relationship would be doomed
while the woman is in a "warm" state of being. He turns and waddles
out the door, ruing the fact that he needlessly drank the entire bottle
of snow-making fluid, when, if he had just let the woman drink
some of it, they could have had a wild and frosty affair.

Dramatis Personae

SLOAN, arachnid-like, lures GARY into her web, all the while visualizing someone else. She has sex with various cast members, smokes, uses profanity, and manipulates everyone in sight, including the director, DONALD, who also plays the producer that defenselessly falls prey to her manipulative arms or legs, whichever they might be. He has sex with her and perhaps JANE, all the while using strong profanity, all the while trying to figure out the truth of the situation, both theatrically and in "reality" while, in addition, he, DONALD, in a desperate attempt at an exculpatory tour de force, plays the role of the wandering "philosopher" who is certain no one is up to any good, and proves it, for the most part, but using overly strong profanity, in our opinion. Simultaneously, CHARLOTTE discusses DONALD out of context with CATHERINE, the director's so-called mentor. She smokes several times and is instructed to cough "engagingly" in the direction of HUGH, a reporter who has sex with GAVIN's unnamed ex-wife (LIBBY) and wrestles with EXPOSITION. Similarly, FLORA plays the associate with whom MICHAEL has sex. ETHEL plays the one with whom he does not, with equal conviction. LYNN, weeping thoroughly, plays the shadowy figure who sees DONALD one last time, as the CREW, CONSULTANTS, and TECHNI-CAL SUPPORT STAFF put down their sandwiches to watch in staged incredulity, bursting the encumbering threads that had heretofore bound them in a repertory of camaraderie and professionalism.

FOR JOHN CLARE & GEORGE GREEN

Poets may love nature, yes
But they *adore* similes, do they not?
Like ravenous locusts set free in golden fields
Of freshly spoken verbiage.

FULL MOON

I find it reasonable this evening
that Otto Leuben,
the *Ripley's Believe It or Not* "German lunatic"
who was supposed to have won a bet
by dealing out a deck of cards in a prescribed order
but only after twenty years of trying
should have inspired an eminently sane poet,
Bob Hershon, to memorialize him
and that through Bob, in a manner of speaking
Otto has spoken to me.

He informed me that it was the time frame
that gave his exploit legitimacy
for had the cards come out right on the first or second try
he would have been derided as a trickster
and then been impelled to establish his lunacy
through more melodramatic undertakings
and thus been incarcerated or worse,
instead of celebrated in the future.
He regretted not having included a "cost of living index"
in the wager, since the sum after twenty years
was barely enough to purchase another deck of cards.
Most astonishing was the realization that I myself
had achieved the very sequence Leuben had been looking for,
and on three occasions: once while idly playing solitaire in 1967;
again, in 1987, when I sailed the cards one by one
into a hat from my cot in a jail cell, as I passed the time
while detained in an unnamed location, in a dream;
and two decades earlier, at the age of eight,
when I tossed a deck of cards
high into the air in a fit of childish frustration
and they fluttered down in no order I was then aware of
but, as the ten of diamonds hit the floor,
completing, as it were, the "deal"
I heard a disembodied Teutonic voice,
the manifestation of which had always been an enigma
until reading Bob's poem:
Vunderbar, mine kint, but I bet
it vill take you tventy years to do it again!

Indirect Homage to Val Lewton

Cat People
Their tongues can get rough.

The Curse of the Cat People
is passed on to their kittens.

I Walked with a Zombie
but only as far as the sacrifice.

Isle of the Dead
Just lie back and relax.

The Bodysnatcher
Keep an eye on yours.

The Seventh Victim
happened to fall on a Sunday.

Shadows in the Dark
How can you tell?

The Leopard Man
He was spotted in the foliage.

The Ghost Ship
It hasn't scared the sharks.

Extraterrestrial Observations

Across the street, Marcia has changed herself into Cindy
and is wearing a dress
that could only have come from Mars
and a hat perhaps suitable for an evening on Neptune.

Up the block, the Moonmen are assembling the ray gun
but there is no cause for alarm — our shack
is sided with Lunarium
under the tarpaper:
their puny devastation beams
cannot get through, cannot alter our equanimity.

Across the street, things have returned to normal —
Cindy has become Marcia again, though her shoes
are apparently from Jupiter, her belt from Pluto.

Let me repeat: the Moonmen's weapons are feeble
and will have *no effect* — on the three-legged chair,
the mildewed curtains, or mar the one-page calendar
that displays the intrepid, pigtailed Miss October
offering a shiny apple month after month —
not the slightest effect at all.

ETHNICITY

Are you Jewish? asked
the elderly Chinese lady at
the dry cleaners my girlfriend
had recommended.
No, I answered.
Because of Rosh Ha-Shanah?
I asked, which was coming up
on Saturday. No answer.
Because of the holiday,
she said, a few seconds later.
My girlfriend's Jewish, I offered,
to make conversation.
Oh, is she very . . . *Religious?*
I supplied; well, she's with *me*, so . . .
She laughed. You *look* Jewish
she observed, as she finally
completed the receipt on the computer.
But you may not want to hear that, she added,
as she misinterpreted my slight surprise.
No, that isn't it, I said, but most people
really don't think so, and, looking for authority
on the subject, I said, accurately if not *correctly*:
Most Caucasians don't think I look Jewish.
Oh, she said cheerfully, then I'm wrong.
When I got home I told my girlfriend
about the Chinese lady at the cleaners.
I thought they were Koreans, she said.

ILLUMINATIONS (DIVERSE MINIATURES)

1. Tableau

The smoke curls steadily upward.
The work of Attila the Hun? No, his "Other,"
Flotilda the Hunnie, cigarette dangling from her lips, braids
bleached in historicity and descending
from the Pannonian past
into the sink of the Pennsylvanian present
where she washes the dishes
to the violins of the rainswept interstate.
On the right, Attila thunders into the driveway
and there, on his right, the more conservative hordes.

2. Impertinence

Like the sun, I endured a turbulent childhood
and became allergic to interstellar dust
while contending with encircling debris
that would have made any entity dizzy, hot,
unstable and content to just float there
and smolder for eons
in a grumpy and extended recovery period
as the center of a gratuitous and onerous "system"
before imploding into cosmic isolation.

3. Big Broadcast of 2005

An important 30-something lawyer
announces confidentially to her cell phone in Duane Park
so that everyone within 30-something feet will know
that Eric Sears tried to screw her; Eric Sears really
really tried to screw her, but it seems that his fiendish
labors had come to naught, so consummately *legal*
had been her slithering.

4. Pasture

"You see," he divulged, "the *nice* thing
about generalized estimating equations . . ."
an exception rings out and the statistician
collapses in a bloody pool of demographics.
This is but the first of the 18,000 possibilities
with which the lecture will conclude,
a factoid that renders much of the audience agog;
the percentage that resists becoming agog
is gently urged toward further improbability.

5. Cenotaph

"Let's say you're an ant
and you have to carry your crumbs
one by one, your breakfast crumbs,
from one side of the vault
to the other side of the vault,"
posited Uncle Silas suddenly to the toaster,
which had begun emitting a faint plume of smoke,
as if on the verge of delivering
an electrifying riposte in the manner of Hester,
Silas's unaccountably absent wife,
but was in reality the result of wistful contemplation
of the agreeable paradise existence must have been
before the imposition of sliced bread.

6. Securities

This investment company is like Van Gogh,
I suppose, because it has found a startling
and idiosyncratic way to invest your funds,
so much so that you will probably hate it,
at first — it will seem repellent and unrewarding
until, prodded by a few inspired analyses
you will come to recognize that
while you were staring at the bottom line
assets had been accruing overhead
so that on retirement you will draw down
an enriching barrage of astonishing perceptions
with which to illuminate the abyss.

7. Prague

At the Franz Kafka Café
I ask for mustard: "No."
Ketchup? "No."
Vinegar? "Doubtful."
Water? "Perhaps."
The waitress has done her homework
and understands perfectly
the connotation of her presence.

8 . Apogee

Having chomped and guzzled our way
to the top of the food chain,
we get to watch the priest, the minister, and the rabbi
take the captured bank robbers
through spectacular Apache country;
and then on to the transcendent afterparty,
where no one can remember: *Is it the Guelfs*
or the Ghibellines that are causing global warming?

9. Gilded Opportunities

You see an innocuous conversation;
we see a virtual cesspool of deceit.
You see a promising business trip;
we see disappointment and ruin.
You see a beguiling landscape;
we see overwhelming doom.
And yet in a slow-motion botanical fireworks
the hibiscus reveals its rarified flower
to us both. You see it fall to the floor
after only a day. Incredibly,
we see it live in glory forever.

10. Vienna

. . . but the vagaries of sunlight have little effect
on the Hapsburgs themselves, as they proceed
methodically from room to room, making minute
adjustments to the dynastic furnishings.
"Something seems always to be a little off," they
opine, "or on the verge of collecting dust."

11. Song of the South

The wind has stopped but the okra is slippery.
Don't take seven types of ambiguity to Florida,
improvise when you get there,
advised Sneaky, our clinically depressed stuffed leopard,
reading the mind of his mute friend, Chilly Steven,
the presumably omniscient bipolar bear.
And now, as if to prove the point
the sun sets with certitude like an overcooked beet
on the poached exteriors,
while the ocean deactivates its liquified turquoise,
the ribbons of asphalt and sand are veiled
and all is perfectly clear.

12. On the River

Several decades ago I observed to someone or other
in an impromptu discussion about poetic *authenticity*
that you could write "I am sailing down the Rhine"
and not be sailing down the Rhine, for example,
and he said: I'm not so sure about that —
so I gave up. As it happens,
I am at present sailing down the Rhine,
even if it is not the river of the discussion
but deeper and colder,
and supports a historical fragment:
for it is the 16th century and there is a surfeit
of vehemence in our picturesque hamlet;
I am taking our excess zeal to market.

13. Gray Gardens

Silent reading came into vogue in the seventh century
but you may still hear words ringing in your ears.
Never mind: open your eyes, is the message,
for who knows? perhaps a band of seraphs
has gathered pictures strange and opulent
and are impatiently awaiting your approval —
unless of course it is *you* who are the suspect passenger
on the indescribable voyage
that is to be detained indefinitely in visual paucity.

14. Modern Times

They are showing excerpts from *The Three Stooges*
during the extended rain delay, because apparently
the complexities of one complete episode
from these devious masters of understatement
might be too *opaque*, too "character-driven"
to hold the cutting-edge attention span
of today's discerning audience.

15. Exposure

"See, in the game of poetry,"
wheezed the old geezer, in a chance assonance
that would not occur again in his lifetime,
"you *never* get dealt a pat hand . . . "
but then they upped the ante
and he had to fold, while the pages of his book
turned indolently in the breeze
and he kicked at the ancient cinders of wisdom
one last time outside their homely tombs
and darkened the air from memory.

16. Alternate Premise

Continue snorkeling in the shallow Jurassic sea
and be entertained by the development
of rudimentary sharks (don't worry, they won't
be ready to bite you for millions of years). Then,
to record a comment, *allegro* or *penseroso*, follow the links
through the aerial blue rectangle or iconic murk, respectively
to the smiling light bulb or brooding cumulo-nimbus cloudlet.
For example: *I have become an ethereal being, and do not know*
my location at any given moment, due to this.
or: *Was there no one on Beekman Place who could break*
the stranglehold that bound them all to wealth and idiosyncrasy?

17. Response

A thousand expostulations
now limp forward
as from a cathartic jewel;
a choice shouts passionately
at other possibilities
until it is followed like a mule
to the shoreline
where intellectual torches
shed light just in time
to stop the sea
of people who are eager
day or night
to resist my call.

18. The Great Game

We explore the plains, forests, mountains
and rivers in search of followers or, on the next level,
zealots. Death means you keep going, only now
you're a zombie. If you take too long to think,
you'll turn into one even quicker. Single zombies
can be neutralized with one or two unsolvable
propositions, but there are different rules
for handling zombie nations
and they are too complicated to explain.

19. Envoy

Someone in the subway filched the hat
from my pocket, through which circumstance
I caught pneumonia in the rain and died.
Is it not curious, I inquire of the other immortals,
that I still speak of such a trivial event
from the armchair of eternity?

SPRING

It started with serial word play. Hebe, a comely body
revolving around the barroom like an asteroid,
makes a momentary stop at the table,
paradoxically reviving "hebetated" senses
with further libations. The more intellectually curious
of the sodden *heb*domad
discussed what day of the week it might possibly be,
until a *hebetudinous* passerby actually tells them,
and then, taking their bewilderment as an invitation,
sits down with his beverage of choice to digress:

A bee has five eyes — one large compound orb
on each side of the head, and three primitive eyes on top
to detect overhead luminosity. Somehow
a beam of light shines from above into the hive
but I cannot detect it. Who am I?

First drinker: *The blood of a honeybee is never sweet,*
if that answers your question.

Second drinker: *The Romans used to feed this sweet*
raisin wine, called something or other, to sick bees
so they'd get well, but you've just got to wonder
if after a while the bees weren't malingering.

Third drinker: *We never drank with our bees*
but it reminds me of when me and the missus,
we'd have Raspberry Jell-O every night for dessert,
except on Saturday, when we'd have Orange —
somehow we liked that one better —
but those euphoric gelatinous days are gone now.

Fourth drinker: *Speaking of women, I always remember the one*
who should have felt more sorry for my long voyage, and
ensuing tribulations, so I would keep mentioning things,
setting up a kind of nest at the base of the relationship,
because I'm sure she was a goddess, the elusive minx,

you should have seen the way she undulated
gleaming and distant
in a nightgown of divinity
against a transparent disk of alabaster clouds.

Fifth drinker: *The bite of a distant woman,*
my grandfather used to say, can be fatal.

Fourth drinker: *It was like being enclosed*
between transcendental commas
and hearing incomprehensible whispers
until I finally nudged the punctuation
but by the time I got to the end of the sentence, she was gone.

Sixth drinker: *It doesn't sound like you were in her breeding group.*

Seventh drinker: *Speaking of futility, the biggest*
butterflies in the world are in "Queen Alexandra's Closet"
and the door to it is in New Guinea
and I went all the way down there
but couldn't get it open. And when I came back
I found that their distant relatives had eaten holes
in the clothes hanging in my own closet,
so I think I learned a good lesson there.

The colloquy was getting too bizarre, even for me
and seeing there would be no answer to the riddle
I left these dubious entities
and their elementary characterization
and took my beverage of choice to a nearby table
where I sat down and composed a sonnet:

Spring

Early in the morning, raindrops on the aluminum dream
and then a replica of the lantern that had guided me
across the platinum night, which included the cypress grove
that had been my gift, and I wanted it back —
but I have to go away now, for tigers and elephants need my help
and after they are helped I will create a waterfall
and rest beside it, and draw up a contract with the adjoining space,
the silver drops of spray blurring its terms and conditions.

But to work out an agreement with these successive vistas
we will need help from a circumference of clarity
and a marvelous pencil to record what is happening. The lake still
needs help; it is far from the actual water. And this is characteristic
of the sort of designer who disappears among the cypresses,
asking the very mildness of the atmosphere for help.

SCENES FOR ALEXANDRA MACPHERSON KELLEY

Now that the hurricane has passed
through our transparent island
and smashed furiously into the resolute molecules of inland air
where at present it is weeping a copious rain in frustration,
let us turn the page, where a gentle *Parkay yellow*
spreads across the enchanted vale
tinged with *burnished kipper* at the edges
and where shadows in *sudden decanted burgundy*
have discreetly spattered the succeeding layout
as if intent on enhancing the already humid village
ingeniously highlighted in *transient blue deep*
and dabbed with *impecunious thatch,* and we hear
quasi-melodious laments in the vernacular, as the villagers
give each other little pieces of their respective minds.
But of course we don't really want to know these people
and since "socializing is networking to no purpose"
we abandon the arrangement and look up
against a background of expectant taupe and reticent gray
to see that an eighty-ton locomotive can float on air,
to watch Japan go through lunar aspirations,
and observe an insecure lobster expiring from self-doubt
on the way to the zoo of scrutiny;
and you can find mystic sights and sounds in your very home
or pass the time in conversation with an atomic clock
but then we see the butterflies
in transcendent orange and immortal black
floating from the mouths of Amish suicides
and can be certain that reality reigns supreme.

Winter Journey

Mist

"O cruel and disconcerting sun,
you should not have disappeared all night
and left my thoughts in shadow;
and you must know that your beloved moon
for these many dark hours
has been lying on her couch, provocative,
and signaling the ships of fate with her jewelry.
If I were a wizard, I would reveal
how you could still gaze upon her
in the diurnal half of infinity
instead of closing her off each day
with compulsive splashes of dawn,
such as those on my window,
and then wondering where she went."

And so farewell sighs the automated voice
as we log off from *nocturnalramblings.com*
to face the pressing questions of the morning:
What can a hula hoop tell us
about managing a portfolio?
How could such a capable architect
get caught between two women?
And: *Was Hedy Lamarr the only Hollywood actress*
who could design naval weaponry?

You see, one day in 1940 Hedy had a conversation
with George Antheil, the avant-garde
composer from New Jersey, about enlarging her breasts.
From this they developed a workable design
for a radio guidance system for torpedoes,
which was not adopted by the Navy at the time, but was
based on a technology that now facilitates cell-phone use.
So, what we would like to know is, if Hedy had had
the genes for larger breasts, would there be *less* dreary
and pointless ambient intrusive yakking on the streets,

or would it merely be louder and even *more* invasive
due to the lack of the abovementioned facilitation?

But we are fingering now the goblet of distraction
and take another heady sip of fleeting erudition,
for since a single shard can date an entire stratum
and yet retain historical respectability,
we will digress and point out
that the Mongols disposed of important prisoners
by rolling them up in rugs and kicking them to death,
or breaking their backs,
or crushing them under floorboards or drowning them
because they thought it was important *not to shed blood*.
YES, IRONY IS WHAT MADE OUR EMPIRE GREAT
intones Genghis Khan from his bottomless tomb.
SURE IT WAS, confirms his son Ogodei,
rolling his eyes in perceptive inebriation
in an early use of italicized sarcasm
as he takes another sip of fermented wisdom
and collapses onto the steppe.

Upstate Sketch

THANKS TO A STEADY DIET OF PERSONAL PRONOUNS
THE DEITIES ARE GAINING WEIGHT, observes the high priest
from the brittle fragment of scroll
I imagine is back there on a neglected shelf
in the Olive Free Library,
while a hypothetical populace mutters in the vernacular
from the part that is missing. More accurately
we are passing the Methodist church on Route 28,
which brings up the pressing question of the afternoon:
Since Art Fry wanted a substance that would keep slips of paper
from flying out of his hymnal
when he was singing in the choir on breezy summer Sundays
was Christianity responsible for the Post-It™ note?
But we urge our vehicle forward,
toward the markets of Phoenicia,
outpacing the triremes on the churning Esopus Creek

70

that bear cargoes of rural paradigms,
dotted lines for the highways,
and impressions of trees bearing fruit
from Troy, Syracuse, Ithaca, and Boiceville
in exchange for the soda pop, journalistic discernment
and comfortable woollen socks
that have brought prosperity and an actual pear tree
for the Phoenician merchant elites
to view with satisfaction
from their almost-Mexican restaurant.
Back in Olivebridge, I reparameterize my scope
to the width of the paradigmatic shed
where just as in my grandfather's day
if you drop a small but crucial metal something
while repairing the red wheelbarrow,
it will elude you on the dusty floorboards
so that the consignment of rusticity
meant to go from here to there will have to stay here
a little while longer — while I take a walk
under the occasional showers north and west of the city
past the Wheel of the Ancients and the Stumps of Prophecy,
the idleness of Garden Zeus and the ominous Fern Forest,
down the Troll Road past the Eternally Shattered Offering
and further, beyond the Paleolithic Beaver Dam
into the disordered stands of leafy entities
and their varying degrees of taciturnity
to the Boulder Overlook and the Stream Going Nowhere,
none of which was identified before I got here;
but the visual evidence I was seeking,
of the hermit thrush,
the most evanescent and inimitable voice in Olive Township
eludes me forever as I approach.

Fertile Crescent Episode

I am the Queen of countless cosmic powers,
used primarily for the exaltation of Inanna
and for this translation by Dr. Annette Zgoll
from the exalted University of Munich,

which is nestled in the dark forests of an unknown land
far to the north and west of my city,
and you can find translations of me
at the Electronic Text Corpus of Sumerian Literature.
So declares En-Hedu-Ana,
the first self-identified poet in history,
although that was not her real name.
She glorified the Moon God, Nanna, and his daughter, Inanna,
although those would not have been their earliest designations.

En-Hedu-Ana herself was the daughter of Sargon of Akkad,
who conquered Sumer along with much else
but since it is said that he was found as a baby
floating in a basket in the river,
clearly Sargon was not what his mother called him at birth.
And so as the boss's daughter Enheduana had a leg up
in the temple priesthood industry, and she worked out of Ur
and wrote hymns and incantations
that were considered sensational.

Temple priestesses, such as those dedicated to Ishtar,
the Babylonian incarnation of Inanna
were functioning prostitutes
that would put out for any male visitor who "donated"
a few coins for the temple's upkeep.

        So alleges *hotbronzeagesluts.org.*

"Listen, Buster, the Moon God might have gotten lucky
from time to time but *you've* got as much chance as a leg of lamb
surviving one of my father's banquets,"
comes Enheduana's gentle reproof. "I didn't *have* to do anything
except put stylus to tablet and write poems
that made the Sumerians feel they were part of the empire,
and my stuff was good enough for the Babylonians
to be digging it half a millennium later. Anyway,
our so-called prostitution was sacred, not the shameless
groveling for chump change the poets of *your* day
elbow each other out of the way to engage in.
And don't think I missed that 'leg up' bit."

Later, I went to find our local Mesopotamian scribe,
the one who sits on his stack of tablets, dozing,
on Chambers Street between the hardware store and the IRT
and bade him set down the following:

Dear Ana,

*Please forgive that I'm dictating this letter, my Akkadian has never been
what it should be. Anyway, you have the most evanescent and inimitable
voice on the Euphrates, but I think you are taking Inanna's "Lady of the
Evening" aspect too literally (she was Ishtar or Venus in later incarnations,
by the way — Frau-Doktor Zgoll can elucidate for you). I think it might
open up your poetic sensibility if you could follow your nocturnal instincts
without the financial ceremony.*

　　　　[signed] *Your admirer from the future*

*P.S. The exotic coins you rejected so scornfully and that may still be lying
scattered there on your bedroom floor, bear the likenesses of my country's
sovereigns, called "presidents," who all used their real names
but were as mythic in their respective ways as your dad!*

　　　　　Further Adventures

So it's 1998 and we're in a Chinese restaurant on Mount Carmel —
no, not California, the original, in Haifa, on the coast
that was briefly under the imperial sway of Sargon of Akkad
and then later part of Phoenicia; no, not the one in Ulster County,
the original — where Elijah's offering of beef
got miraculously overcooked before Ahab and Jezebel —
I mean in *front of* Ahab and Jezebel, while that of the chefs of Baal
remained like unsliced Carpaccio, and so Elijah cooked their goose.
But none of this appears on the menu and our waitress,
who is from Thailand, inquires if we're Americans
and, when we say yes, asks if we could please explain
the meaning of two English words. Sure, we say, what are they?
Extravaganza and *toady.*

Our answers were less interesting than the question
or that she foreshadowed the upcoming government —
ours not hers. I could have seen the omens on that very day

had I performed an augury on the stir-fried beef
(known to the Romans as sinobovomancy),
that America would be scourged by avarice and deceit
while plagues of toadies, hacks, shills, and flunkies
laid down an extravagant smokescreen of misdirection.
The unquenchable greed and resolute bigotry
would have confounded Genghis Khan,
who not only indulged in religious toleration
but squandered massive quantities of capital
on needlessly promoting the prosperity of the average citizen.

But don't get me started . . .
Because it's almost time to stop
interjects the automated voice from *inevitability.com* —
and obey the law of the setting sun, I imagine,
that compulsive darkener of what is already in shadow,
and retire to my idiosyncratic estate,
which brings up the final question of the night:
Since in the olden days a few sips of a rum-and-something
with a vibrant chunk of lime
was enough for me to swim with all the endorphins I needed,
so that when I emerged and sauntered down the shore
toward the hazy metropolis, the present extended indefinitely,
even though time was discreetly devouring my footprints
so that there was no way to get back . . .

but the phantoms of digression have assisted the answer
in eluding my thoughts, which have been intercepted
by the rising moon and the sparkle of her jewelry,
which could lead me down the trail to Parthia
or to introduce further anachronism
to the court of the Great Khan,
or otherwise continue the long campaign.

MISPRISION

someone said Sappho could be understood
only through her original tongue
and I said I didn't think so
as educational as that would probably be

someone wrote that Charles VIII
entered France in the 1490's
and I said to myself: I don't think so
he was born many years before that
but he did penetrate Italy in 1494
as far as Naples, and didn't withdraw
for an entire year, which seems extraordinary
by today's standards
but he finally lost virility and everything else
by hitting his head on a doorway in 1498

someone wrote that gardening was a literature
in which scholars nibbled at the edges
of what appeared to be an insurmountable edifice
and I thought: that makes perfect sense
nibbling is an authentic scholarly pursuit
and eventually the edifice will get lower
and can be surmounted

somebody said that cretins painted murals
and got out of labyrinths but that seems unlikely
and someone wrote to say it's time for a poetry museum
but I don't understand how anyone could possibly know that
and isn't that what our books are already
glassless vitrines
where you're allowed to run your fingers over the art
or nibble on the implications
or loiter in the white passageways between the lines
hoping to meet the lenders to the exhibition

Out and Around

The streets have never been more profligate
with automotive self-assertion. The sun
has its instructions: keep up the heat. Nouns
float about like paper. Some of them orate,
creating haphazard currents of parallel realities
and on the corner stands the archetypal critic, musing,
as if in a blog — scanning the heavens
for discourse, projects, process, and praxis
while poetry pauses, unnoticed, to signify
on his or her leg. And since we are not on the same page
I turn it and move on to the window of Barnes & Noble
where *The Austro-Hungarian Empire for Dummies*
is on display, justifying the years of toil spent
in bringing *La Monarchie austro-hongroise pour les gourdes*
to the anglophone market;
and somewhere else in a more strenuous context
the grizzlies are creeping closer
and are doing well from the outside
but can they prosper in the paint
is the query put to the otherwise empty landscape,
and a gentle ripple of opinion
passes through a waving field of experts.
But you are skeptical of all this darting about, you say.
Very well, I shall pick my way through the fundamentals
in these explosive times and relate a sad but cohesive tale:
Krakatoa grew up with two magmas,
which created feelings of stress, conflict, and volatility
and it resulted in a predictably eruptive displacement
that preempted the attention of all in the neighborhood —
and thus they were witness to monumental trauma
as acted out with rock and gas,
supported admirably by lava and all the ash you could ask for.
Now, let us return to the unfinished landscape:
You are correct that the lesson is not clear,
the translation inadequate, the rainbow suspended.

ELSEWHERE

DO YOU REMEMBER WHEN WE DODGED SHOWERS OF POISONED ARROWS
OR WHEN THEY SET THOSE PIGS ON FIRE AND SENT THEM SQUEALING LIKE CRAZY
INTO THE MIDST OF OUR WAR ELEPHANTS, WHO WERE TRUMPETING LIKE CRAZY
AND OUR GUYS WERE FALLING OFF THE ELEPHANTS AND NOT GETTING UP?

AND DO YOU REMEMBER WHEN THEY THREW POTS FULL OF SERPENTS
THAT BROKE ON THE DECKS OF OUR SHIPS, AND EVERYONE JUST WENT NUTS
AND THE SNAKES WERE LIKE HANGOVERS FROM THE GODS MADE MANIFEST
AND WE TOOK OFF OUR ARMOR, JUMPED OVERBOARD AND SWAM TO SHORE?

AND REMEMBER WHEN WE CATAPULTED BAGS OF SCORPIONS INTO
THEIR CAVALRY AND THEN THREW JAVELINS DIPPED IN VENOM
AND OUR SLINGERS HURLED STONES INSCRIBED WITH DEROGATORY PHRASES
THAT BOUNCED SARDONICALLY OFF THE HELMETS OF THEIR INFANTRY?

THOSE WERE GOOD TIMES. FOR OUR CAUSE WAS AS JUST AS THEIRS WAS
AND THE SELF-ROASTED PORK DELICIOUS AFTER EVERYTHING
HAD CALMED DOWN AND THOSE WHO WERE DYING
FINALLY STOPPED COMPLAINING ABOUT IT . . .

A burst of empathic marmalade spatters the English traveler
as he peruses these ancient adventures,
and a lion of sorts springs across his brow
and frightens off the spirit that had nurtured his boredom.

Adjacently, two sparkling young ladies paint the carriage window
to reflect the inclusion of their faithful celestial dog
to whom the clutter of earthly landscape is irrelevant
as he trots off to investigate a notional empyrean

and other items have been removed
to allow our spectator to concentrate
on the drawing room door, where we will leave her
for to stay longer would cause comment,

and I, too, am on the wrong side of a portal,
kept from warmth and civilized appurtenance
through another distracting quatrain fashioned
from exile in the hallway of misadventure

and I never noticed the offbeat zodiac high on the wall,
how the dog seems ready to pounce on the trilobite
though they are millions of paint specks apart;
well, maybe not millions, and I am privileged to have a book

in my wearisome circumstance on the metallic cushion of stairs
and I can finally read about the Parthians
who didn't pay enough attention and became Sassanians,
a process I now understand at least as well as they did

for they too had left their keys hanging in the past
and were caught in the future without them
so that fate was left completely in charge of their mortal details
until they came to ask: what was the present after all

but regret for the past or anxiety about the future,
there was no time "now" to actually achieve anything
and thus they sidestepped their continuance like avoiding
a bag of scorpions, and were swept off into the advancing moment

but I will disturb you no further while you are dreaming
on one of the other shelves beneath our common roof,
floating there on metaphysical contrivance
as echoes tumble into inaudible perspective

and as if our travellers had any chance at all
of reaching a satisfactory destination
where the lion would not himself fall asleep
and the dog not return with news of a further eternity.